Praying in Indian Country

Cynthia Poten

Avid Readers Publishing Group
Lakewood, California

The opinions expressed in this manuscript are those of the author and do not represent the thoughts or opinions of the publisher. The author warrants and represents that she has the legal right to publish or own all material in this book. If you find a discrepancy, contact the publisher at www.avidreaderspg.com.

Praying in Indian Country

All Rights Reserved

Copyright © 2014 Cynthia Poten

This book may not be transmitted, reproduced, or stored in part or in whole by any means without the express written consent of the publisher except for brief quotations in articles and reviews.

Avid Readers Publishing Group

http://www.avidreaderspg.com

ISBN-13: 978-1-61286-226-2

The author has singular use of the art images in this book. The etchings, and the photographs of them, are under copyright by the artist, and are not to be reproduced or sold without written permission from the artist. Contact: maryprisland@yahoo.com

Printed in the United States

For my Mother and Father

Contents

I
Shape Shifter	1
Mother Hawk	2
In the Winter of 1774	4
A Quantum of Wonder	5
Eden	6
The Guiding Star	7
Listening	8
A Place with No Trees	9
The Gulls Their Lonely Cries	10
Chasing Fireflies	11
Before the Shuffle	12
Bradford 1947	13
In the Wellfleet Woods	14
Liking Each Other	15
The Engine Soundfile	16
And Every Town and City	17
Wondering in Central Park	18

II
There's an Eddy Current	23
The Spirits of Mannahatta	24
The Old Ones of Shokan	25
Underground Sun	26
Macedonia Brook	28
At the Center of the World	29
Praying in Indian Country	30
The No-Souls	31
Tracking the Ancestors	32
August Requiem	34
River of Kites	35
Jeanerette's Spring	36
Guatemala Twilight	37

Nurse from America   38
Feathered Alignment   39

III

Pebbles   45
Hour of the Marigold   46
Cross Country Sketches   48
For Troy Davis   49
November 11, 2008   50
High Noon   51
Piece of America's Heart   52
A Strange Flag   53
Notes on a Christian War   54
Who Were You?   55
Guantanamo   56
The Drone Masters   57
Calling Mercy   58
Stitching   59

IV

The Alchemy of Light   65
The Turtle   66
Pay Nanusurukam, Pay Nanuavahkam   67
The Language of Trees   68
Before I Knew the Words   69
Their Voices Came Later   70
A Silver Hum   72
For Leonard Peltier   73
Mortal in the Forest   74
Opalescent Mirror Dream   75
Climate Icons   76
The Lobster   77
Sipping as One   78
Why There is Laughter   80
The Quail are Frolicking on My Roof   81

The Mandrill   82
A Fly Story   84
A Cesium Sea   86

V

Waking up in the Infinite Plan   91
Her Lichen Eyes   92
To Tongore Creek   93
Tso'Noma Song   94
Insectival Buzz   95
Diary with Lime and Magenta   96
Klamath River Tao   98
Rain Woman   99
In the Canyon   100
Their Wings Made No Sound   101
Animal Trust   102
Love Song in A Minor   103
In Full Leaf   104
Petals   105

I

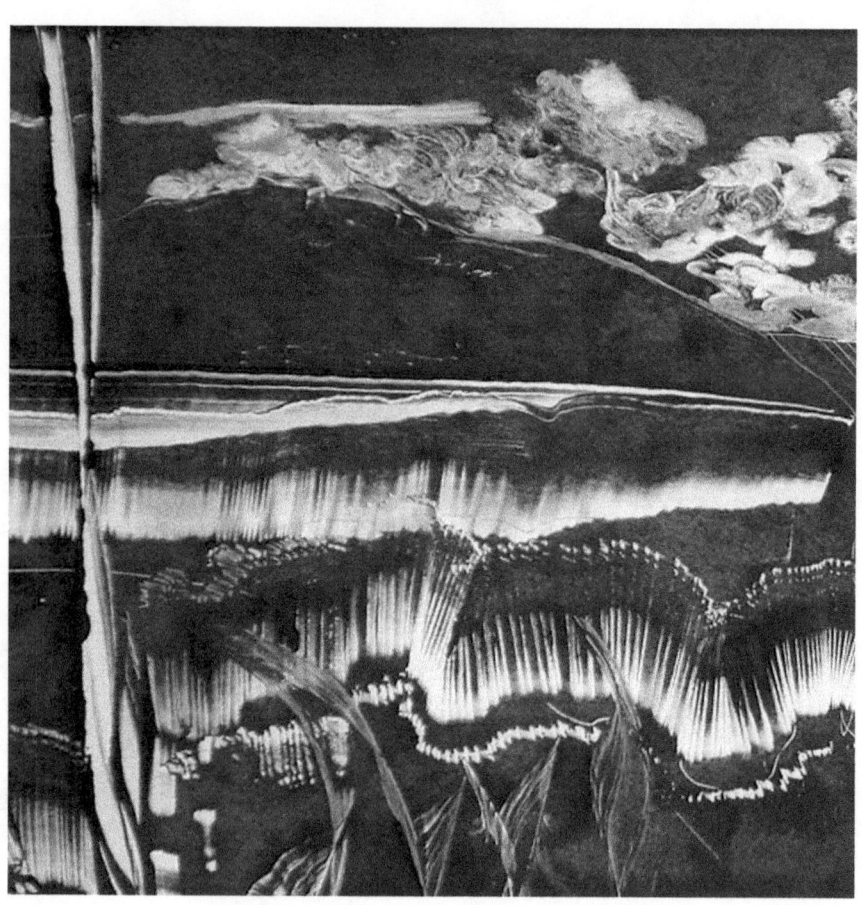

In the flickering mirror of time all events quiver in layers
Each tree, each trigger of grass,
each small and large wave of water will reveal the raw story

Joy Harjo
an excerpt from *Returning from the Enemy*

Shape Shifter

A moth
with the coppery iridescence of an Apache pot
made of mica clay and fired the ancient way
skips from puddle to puddle
sipping obsidian waters
wing flame wing
flame

Mother Hawk

I lie me down by the river
Warm sand quiets my mind
Warm sand and the river drum
heartbeat of water on water on stone
pulses of rustle and swish

She calls from a blue arc above
a long bright rasp with a thin edge
a razor slice of almost song
She calls and that bright edge is a portal

I'm belly down on her back now
gripping silk feathers, riding a resinous wind
marveling at the clarity of the water
at being able to see the dark spine
of a salmon swimming upstream

I don't see the salmon's aura
the way I imagine she does
the way I imagine she sees every shift
in earth's light show of Being
the gold violet flares of two women
walking down the bar
how they startle sparrows into orange sparks
streaking away from a lime glow of willow
how the women's flares become still
before merging into a rainbow haze
of bodies sprawled on the riverbank
chatter sifting into the air like chimes,
silvery echoes that fade as we rise on a warm current
.

She's flying now, heading downriver, her body steady
despite the powerful thrust of her wings
When she lands on a snag, I slide off her back
and descend a maze of charred branches
confident I can find my way home
only to discover the last branch is 20 feet above ground.
I don't mind though
sitting there swaying in pine whisper

until a chainsaw erupts, its brazen whine a cue
for thoughts to reemerge, almost like chronic pain
thoughts of war, wars on trees, wars for oil
wars on the heart at the center of the earth
wars wrapped in white phosphorous, depleted uranium
and why, why men create so many perversions of fire
to turn the shimmer of life to ash

Ah but she's back now, gripping my perch with her talons
settling in beside me, taking my breath away
I keep my eyes cast down for fear she'll change her mind
but her great soft wing enfolds me
We become one breath on a black branch
and waves of green flow all around

In the Winter of 1774

my DNA shivered in the young twigs
of a New England family tree, white oak
they thought they were, strong and already tough
from the transplant to a wild new land
They're white ash now, kept in a Christian urn

Christmas was wrapped in early colonial that year.
snow wandered the cobblestone streets
drifted the narrow cart lanes
muffled the alarm of ax blows in bare woods

West of the Great Divide
the shortest day had closed its narrow door
A new cycle of light unfolded in slivers
Snowdrifts mounded the plains
Fierce winds froze the wild rivers

The fire gods kept their promises
Logs blazed in circles of stone
Shadows danced on painted skins, on pale adobe walls
Warm blood slept in burrows and dens

Other gods, nameless to those
who would change all this
had colder promises to keep
the still life of snakes, the binding of sap
the biding of root and spore and seed

For some it was a time of hunger
for some a time of stories
but for all it was one pulse
one body held in what seems, looking back
the mothering arms of the Holy
in what seems looking forward
a promise we are being asked to keep

A Quantum of Wonder

comes with being born, like our tiny fingernails
that begin as damp petals and become pink shells

like wheeze-snorting deer in the midnight corn
or stars stringing beads in the dark of the moon.

Wonder doesn't know power mind looming, you
know the one--arrogant, toxic, bristling with violence

the one that grinds and schemes the whole rushed
day, the paleface captive night. No, wonder waits

open, silent, like a first-day squash blossom
dewy and crisp, trembling with gold dust for bees

sprouting hopes like furred antlers or ancillary fins
like invisible molars chewing roots into pliancy

for the weaving of all we can gather, thistledown
and coils of light, the cords of blood that bind us

on our knees to the innocent deer, the infinite plan
all for the weaving, always the weaving

baskets of praise, and wings, strong wings to soar
the torn ethers, broken prairies and charcoal trees

fanning heart wings into zephyrs of healing
of careful giving back for all we have taken

as if we were shamans, as if our once wild ears
were still wide open to what the holies say

Eden

Running down hill
little foot after little foot
on stubbled grass
avoiding the apple drops
aware of eyes all around
especially the laden trees,
she doesn't see the snake
his smooth black scales
his forked red tongue
until he stops
directly in front of her
asks, why the hurry

I love to run, she replies
Why are you here

I'm here every day, child
I live in this garden

I'll bring you a present then
she says, not moving
because she likes the snake
and wants to know
when she might see him again
But the snake slips away
a faint shift in the grass
Her ears become caverns
Every leaf has an echo
even the fruit on the ground

The Guiding Star

From the foot of my bed
I could see across the hall into the dim parlor
The player piano was a mirror of tree lights
shining in balsam air
My father stood in his coat

She had no fire? my mother asked
No, the house was freezing
that's what took me so long
I came back for wood
And the girl?
Asleep, poor thing
She has no presents for her

I didn't see the star guiding my mother's hands
to the doll carriage meant for me
He took it and turned
Wait, she said, unwrapping a present
Take this robe
I'll make you another one

I can still see the doll carriage
not how it looked in the tree lights
but when I discovered it
in the back of the closet
I can't see the girl
but I still see her blonde mother's face
the day the war ended
streaked with tears because she knew
her husband would come home

Everything felt bright that day
like the aftermath of a hurricane
Up and down the street
people hung toilet paper streamers
from their windows

Listening

So early the ominous edge
quilted from talk scraps of a distant war
At night the sirens piercing the dark
The droning worry of planes

Our town on the coast south of Boston
had an army base, a possible target for German subs
On blackout nights my mother read pioneer tales
After I heard about the baby who died of diphtheria
I didn't want to listen any more
stayed by the window checking the tape
that sealed the shade against the frame

Good days men reeled the mackerel in
loud cries for the big ones
all strung together and lowered
into a murky tide
sloshing against the pilings
We lay on our bellies
around a fish hole cut in the pier
tugging at roped fish
listening to excited gulls

A Place with No Trees

Driving into Boston
four of us in the back seat
I have a window, being second oldest
and almost nine
We go through an underpass
arc around a high wall of concrete
and whssssh, everything is concrete
looming, ominous
and where are the trees
I lean back in the seat and close my eyes

When I open them, the world is the same
a river of carshine rushing along
buildings blocking the sun
everything as it was before
except a feeling like falling
and I don't know where I'll land
and it doesn't feel safe
a place with no trees

Gulls Their Lonely Cries

Past the schoolhouse the climb begins
At the top of the hill the bay unfurls
boats rocking and gulls their lonely cries
the sun streaming sounds of wind and tide
the golden eye daisy an altar for bees
and the meadow so green and a sit-on stone

Heading home, tufts of green in the sidewalk
and a path in the woods, a little woods really
but large to young eyes and dim and the shock
of seeing the little boy tied to a tree
his tormenters circling sticks aloft, their voices shrill

Running fast 'til the cross street forces a stop
and finally the park, feet skimming over the green
a wide green mowed to the tennis court fence
where the big kids have their laughing time
and the balls their soft hollow clops
and the pigeons are so nonchalant

Chasing Fireflies

We were a nation of backyards and fences
Sparrows flown in by God skipped songs
into our shared pool of air
spreading bright circles of sound
to remind us we belong to each other

Love came to us that way
but we were puzzled by the fences
we couldn't see, the ones that kept us
from running after balls next door
Why can't we, we wanted to know
The answer never made sense
made us a little uneasy

which we forgot as we fell asleep
parent murmur drifting up the stairs
while we ran free as foxes in our dreams,
chasing fireflies all the way to Main Street
through everyone's backyard

Before the Shuffle

Any morning and all around a welcoming
even the pavement damp with blueshine
The air as wide as imagine
sunlight sweeping across the pond
with a robin's song, as my feet move on
the mile to school a secret gift
time to swim in the shimmer
before the shuffle, the coat hook and bell
the pledge of allegiance, the drills to reason
the confounding puzzle of history
each odd intricate piece staking a claim
in the fields and forests of my mind

Bradford 1947

Empty milk bottles waited on the front porch
to enter the rhythm of horses and men
Hammers and roosters sang in the same choir
Three mornings a week the wagon came
and every day the last white sips of Europe's
old mandala slipped into the Before time
when towns formed the outer edge of survival
and farms were a link to the center of earth
people and animals walking the four directions together
while the After time waited in crates at train stops
near Boston and other places we'd come to know
places where a harness was only a metaphor
because the unpacking never stopped
and stairs were for tenements and fire escapes
because rooms with a view
were too high to reach by foot

In the Wellfleet Woods

I was shuffling gold October leaves
    that traced the old King's Highway,
a trail well-traveled long before
    any idea of kings arrived -- by deer and
bears, by lynx and fishers, bobcats and cougars
    and foxes, by centuries of moccasins
tuned to the pulse of the forest --
    when something I can't explain occurred ...

...We had to flee, our village in flames
We stayed off trail in a moonless dark
    When the crack of gunfire grew faint
we felt we were safe for the moment
    They thought we moved without sound
but their ears were muffled in lies
    We moved with sound

...then I felt myself slogging
    through snowmelt,
mud on my skirt, a bucket of embers
    in my hand, heading for the cabin
where an infant died of fever

Liking Each Other

We left home at an early age
It was a nest we outgrew anyway
or it fell apart in an argument
Any road led to any city then
When we got to the streets
the dust was different, powdery, like ash
Each day was new and the same
In the factory a halo of dust
smelled acrid and strangely sweet
We never forgot that halo
Two summer-job girls and full-timer
women with cigarette voices
wrapping boxes and liking each other
The song said walk on
walk on with hope in your heart
and you'll never walk alone
There were days this was true
Faces smiled over empty bottles
and sideways sometimes on a train
Faces still pass in the dark, ever more
faces, my eyes closed but not asleep

The Engine Sound File

Motor vibrations advanced on our minds
wave upon wave they entered the ear canals
planting racer perceptions and a runaway pulse

In the unpaved forest, trucks moved slowly
crackling the leaves, almost sneaking past
the evening's chorus of crow caws
the scurry of quail in dry grass

In the village cars passed in hushes
and after, morning rushed in all cheeps
and jay calls, the woodpeckers working
trees creaking their branches
waving their leaves

In the suburbs the pattern became
a matter of streets, how leafy they were
how large and planted the yards
how broad the ratio of porous to paved

In the cities the advance was complete
wave upon wave without end, an ocean
of engines and men so constant we ceased
to notice our immersion in the construct

The elaborate perpetual motion stretched
behind us and beyond as we pressed on
pausing to listen to fountains, waiting for
warblers in quiet corners of a park

And Every Town and City

seemed an outpost of desire
wrapped in trees that cradled the birds
and shaded the streets
the black reliable streets
amalgamated tar and granular resist
angular here, meandering there
but always linear beckoning
And who understood
that pavement is a grave?

There never was a funeral
We never carved her name
we just walked on, or rode
in sleek machines
that sped us from the past
into the right here right now
the very any place desire led us
while what we wanted ran ever ahead
an unsuspected scout of paved imaginings

Wondering in Central Park

Heading for the zoo
our conversation was a slow meander
little streams pouring their hearts out
almost giddy with release from yesterday's canal
all those years of channeling
funneling into culverts
silently slipping under asphalt

We never forgot swimming naked
in the pool where the diversion began
how cool and glossy black it was
shaded by newcomer trees
no hint of the ancient forest
or the ancient Lenape who walked it
following the river all those many miles
to the sea, leaving their crops to ripen
returning laden with dried fish

In the churchyard alien shrubs
emerged from streetlights into Sunday morning
little sentries clipped and rounded
guarding the cement walk to a door
we never entered, because where to pray
was a prickly question that drove us to wander
and when we didn't wander, we felt trapped

Sometimes we saw water shining on a table
or sat by a pond where water lilies told us
that nothing fully sensed is ever lost
Life moved us along in this way
beyond the grasping fist that doesn't know itself

We were almost at the Zoo when a man yelled
You are God. And *you* are God we said
noticing, how odd, his dachshund was on a skateboard
The man hastened by, the back of his head
balding in a circle like a medieval monk's

II

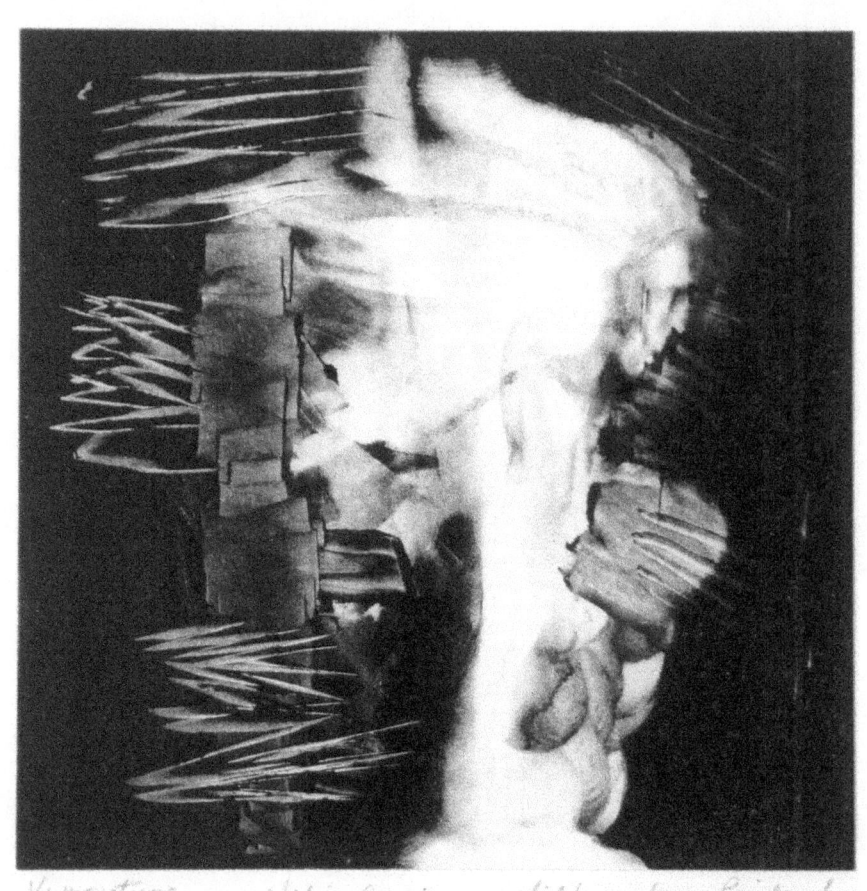

1/1 monotype Native American & child Mary Prisland

To begin remembering our Indigenous belonging on the Earth back to life we must metabolize as individuals the grief of recognition of our lost directions, digest it into a valuable spiritual compost that allows us to learn to stay put without outrunning our strange past, and get small, unarmed, brave, and beautiful.

Martin Prechtel
from *The Unlikely Peace at Cuchumaquic*

There's an Eddy Current

in the
river of remember
It flows upstream awhile
carries us
to that silky pass
between uprush and down
where the fishes wait

The Spirits of Mannahatta

The heart of a Buddhist Kalachakra ceremony
is the creation of a sand mandala dedicated
to individual and world peace.

When the Dalai Llama decided
to hold a Kalachakra in America,
an early question was where --
a peaceful country setting or Manhattan?
The city, it was decided.
More people would be able to attend.

An American devotee of Buddhism
assisted the Lamas in organizing the details.
One of the first steps
was to visit the Spirits of Mannahatta
and ask their permission.

I was stunned when he told me this.
I'd assumed the native spirits
had long since fled the city,
driven elsewhere by the concrete
the subways, the cables, the sewers.
Oh no, he explained, they can't
be driven away, they *are* this place.

The Lamas went to the deepest
subway station on the island.
At first the Spirits seemed angry
at being summoned, but once they
understood the Lamas' purpose, they said yes.

The Old Ones of Shokan

They live in the creek rushing on.
They whisper as the sun rains west
glazing copper leaves cast like cobbles
on mowed slopes of burnished grass
They laugh in stone-walled groves of pine
and towering hemlock
pleased the plowed fields are no more
They hide in the mountains
where storms crack wild on the peaks
and night's suede drums
make harmonies of hungry blood
its soft lipped chitters and calls
its beak-edge hoots and low whistles
And after you've closed your tent flap
drifted down deep into new moon sleep
the cries they left in time's branches
will startle your dreams

Underground Sun

Enter the cave, she says, and keep going.
With each step away from daylight
shed one more thing you think you want.

I walk past campfire remains into a gauzy dusk
stepping over nest litter and tiny bones.
As darkness envelops, there's a shift in the air,
the cave taking me in.

Turn on your flashlight, and don't look back.

The cave becomes a deep surround of cliffs and
ledges. Flats and dunes bear the imprint of waves,
of runnels and ripples, old eddies and pools.

Now you must stop, turn off the light and don't move.

Earth's hum is different here -- fainter, lower.
Are the tremors my trepidation?

Soon I'm flowing over rocks
echoing under bridges that span the years
I didn't know uncertainty is grace.
The year I was a leaf on a branch
dancing in reflections
from the river I would drown in.
The year I was a flock of snowflakes
riding an errant wind,
a clump of parsley still green in a frozen garden.
The year I stood O Palestine
near barbed wire and armed guards
watching your olive trees burn
black smoke where the sun used to shine.

Use the torch now and move forward

The tunnel narrows, presses down from above.
I crouch, hold my arms close
brush against stone.
Far ahead of me there's a glow.
I can see without the torch
and soon I can stand

The cave opens into a chamber
where light pours into a central fire pit
like the visitation of a God.

I regret I have nothing for starting a fire
nothing to burn as an offering, so I kneel
and kneeling, I suddenly realize
is what I wanted all along.

Macedonia Brook

Right here is where I'll pitch my tent
here on your soft bank, Macedonia, my head due North
aimed at your foamy rush through blue boulders
your silvery glide through the night
I'll listen to your cool, playful bubbling
soothing the firestorms of this age
pushing far from this dark hour
the stones we've cast, the first and the last
sizing them down, rounding them down
until they are a fine dark sand
gathered at the edge of time
waiting for the imprint of a pipit foot
a deer hoof, a raccoon's clever hand
waiting for a fisherman to net a plump untainted trout

At the Center of the World

It was the time of the new millennium
The tides flung human feet on America's shores
only feet, tied into shoes

It was the time of Kogi elders walking barefoot
from the mountains to the sea
wearing hand-woven robes like a sacrament
crossing the rope bridge that kept them safe from history

It was the time of ceremony rising
From sacred graves and concrete streets
from prison cells and poisoned lands
curls of blue smoke sweetened starlit air

It was the time of justice calling back its tongues
its native tongues
(for how can they remember
if they have no tongue?)

But they remember
They know why the rain doesn't fall,
or falls in floods, why plants and animals disappear
and they know the medicine

It was the time of butterfly jaguars
of elephants grieving
The Pacific cradled its burdens
Hurricanes whipped the Atlantic

It was the time of kneeling
of seeding unplowed soil

Praying in Indian Country

I go to the Rock hoping I'm ready
I hauled the wood, long years of wood
still wet with tears and prayers
and still I cry even as I climb
It's all I can do to show my regret

Will they take pity then
the Spirits who live in these mountains
Will they listen to my Anglo words
show me the path?

A girl hands me crocus bulbs
and points to a place for their planting
But wait, I say, that spot is paved
Maybe the lawn but not by the stone
My home is not a grave, not yet

I'm in an empty greenhouse now
with the cringing man who betrays
Is this the harvest of his blind disdain
the tool shed almost empty too
sunlight slanting through the glass
an old banker pillowed up in bed
wrapped in a quilt and an iphone

I walk a cool night sky immense with stars
still with the man who betrays
There's a bright light on the horizon
Is it the moon? No, it's a jet
dreamily rising as gravity blinks

And Earth is a green map
covered with lines the color of blood
O no, the man cries
Explosions rip through the sky
The map dissolves in a slow dry rain
Flashes of shrapnel spin in pink dust

The No-Souls

The Lenni Lenape chief says
there are two kinds of people on Earth
those with Souls and those without.

It's 1993. He's speaking to a small gathering
of Delaware River activists.
Only so many Souls can exist on earth

at any one point in time, he explains.
At this time there are more no-Souls, which
means there will be more and more no-Souls

because the child of two no-Souls is always
a no-Soul and the child of a Soul and a no-Soul
is always a no-Soul.

A middle-aged psychologist is incensed.
What can that mean? she demands, is there
no redemption for the no-Souls?

He looks at her with dark penetrating eyes.
It's not a question of redemption, he replies.
The air is turbulent with questions.

How did this begin, this proliferation of no-Souls?
And why? And if it's true, what can this mean
for the future of human life on earth?

The Lenape chief does not provide answers.
It seems his intention is simply
to put the idea out there.

I see him yet, a short man of noble demeanor
standing tall and calm in his regalia.

Tracking the Ancestors

For a kid with no grandparents
there wasn't much to go on
I saw my mother's father once when I was two
a big smile above a big belly
pink balloons in one hand, a cane in the other
He died of gangrene that year

I followed a faint track on my mothers side
Her mother was a widow
who raised seven Victorian girls
They washed their petticoats by hand
in a boarding-house laundry room
Each had at least three
On Sundays they rode to Haverhill
in an open wagon, wearing white dresses
tied at the waist with red ribbons

That trail was a dead end she discovered in England
claiming she was told they must have been Jews
who changed their name when they came here
in the late 1700s, a time of anti-Semitism
when poverty was a crime
On my father's side there was no trail at all

I dream them floating above the Atlantic
spectral, undulating faces, marbled with immigrant hope
skeletal hands raking the cobalt waves
Were they victims too of the puritan stain
Did they know what they erased
when they left for a land that wouldn't know who they were

I dream a dark wall of buildings mid-air
all chiseled stone, some flat roofed, some dormered
six stories of windows, three stories, four
A clock-tower pierces raw clouds
It could be London or Belfast
There are no couples holding hands

no children rolling hoops
no elders leaning on canes
just buildings aloft in overcast air
I want the sun to rise above the rooftops
or set behind me, casting bits of gold
on the blank window panes

One day I feel them watching
through my children's eyes
So what should I do, I ask
about the continent between my children
and their grandparents

*Never mind that now. just watch over
watch carefully, guard the life strings
glowing round them as they run*

August Requiem

Young boys on a San Diego beach
run in and out of shallow waves
back and forth over the wet sand,
their high excited voices merge
with the hushing surf

Hear.. O.. she.. ma, they cry out
Hir o shi ma they seem to be calling
oh can you hear us, oh Hir o shi ma.
can you hear how little we know

The impossible strangeness of this
coming at me as I watch the boys play
The clear vowels lodged in my brain
as firmly as acorns in years of mast
sprouting an echo of the day
that mercy hides from children

River of Kites

The children run their kites aloft
near the edge of a canyon
kites they painted and glued
and tied with bright streamers
There are frog and polar bear kites
salmon and panther and honey bee kites
animal friends who are disappearing
though they don't quite grasp what this means
They only know they want to help the animals
so they breathe carefully on each kite
before they run it aloft

When a kite sails high enough to fly on its own
they cut it loose
Soon a great wind arrives
and tucks itself under the kites,
carries them far beyond the canyon
People hurry out of their houses
stop their cars to watch
Trains and buses halt between stations
Everyone wants to see the river of kites in the sky

Backlit by the sun
the kites are a giant shadow puppet
a many colored dragon
whose bright shadow dapples the rivers
the smoky towns, the patches of trees
the fields ablaze in late day sun

Jeanerette's Spring

Perhaps if I'd stayed behind
And lived it bomb by bomb
I might have grown up at last
And learnt what is meant by Home
                              Derek Mahon

The poet left Belfast and walked on into the world
like so many of us
our lives a journey from place to places
where home becomes a state of mind
and of body, the knowing body
the refuge under the skin
that passes for home wherever we are

It can be random, this home, something
I might remember massaging the soles
of my feet after a long shower
Sometimes it's a contented sigh
from the back of the left knee
or a smile in the right arm after eating
wild mushrooms

Once it was a fluttering sweetness
in my solar plexus
That was when I sipped from Jeanerette's spring
near the sacred mountain ledge
where she later lifted her tattooed face in prayer
and burned raisins as an offering

Once it was a clutch in the heart
the day I watched the little guy sent to school
with a dirty face, how his tense and pleading need
made the other kids uneasy

That need, that urgent need
so immense in this world of refugees
homes gone by bomb and by fiat
learning what is meant by Exile

Guatemala Twilight

We sit on a narrow balcony, tufted cobbles shaded soft below
The day's heat slows, worn stones sigh
wilted leaves revive
Sipping bottled water, we drift with the languorous clouds
sheets of shimmering peach
billows of wedgewood blue

You can't imagine, she says
a little grandmother came into the clinic
carrying three children
all of them dehydrated, full of parasites
After we injected fluids
worms crawled out of their eyes
Thinking them dead the poor woman screamed
and ran out the door
When she came back in a truck to bring them home
she saw they were still alive
but only barely
The family will gather on a dirt floor
to watch them die under a naked light bulb

A delivery truck clatters into the courtyard
scattering our silent, useless sorrow
Diesel fumes drift up the bougainvillea
A short, thin guard in uniform jumps from the truck
and shoulders a semi-automatic
The trees are black silhouettes now
The driver carries cases of beer through a dark doorway

Nurse from America

The Mayan women walk in rubber sandals
over grassy foot paths and dirt roads
over cobblestones and weedy concrete
They arrive at the clinic before the door opens

In the windowless waiting room
they are a garden of skirts and shawls,
bright embroidered blouses
Their voices rise and fall
sparrow chat, dove murmur
soft ripples from shaded streams
flowing around a silent elder with tired eyes
that easily flare into smile

When a mother arrives with a limp infant
in her arms, the nurse sees her next

In the back courtyard
a two-year-old plays with sticks
He makes no demands on his mother
who takes patient histories
listening in Mayan, writing in Spanish

He wanders into the makeshift kitchen
for a drink of water
Back in the courtyard he falls asleep in the grass

Every evening the nurse sweeps the rooms
straightens the benches, the chairs
replenishes open shelves of supplies
Early in the morning she washes the floors

Feathered Alignment

When gun point ideologies
breathe their final blood stained sigh
and the glare of mourning the broken world
fades to a darkling pink
the way white petals sometimes do

When greed has crushed the last bed of ferns
held in feathered alignment
by only a faintly wind in the once was forest
will we remember then to follow the child
whose holy wild could lead us home?

III

There was no end to it; it knew no boundaries; and he had arrived at the point of convergence where the fate of all living things, and even the earth, had been laid ... The lines of cultures and worlds were drawn in flat dark lines on fine light sand, converging in the middle of witchery's final ceremonial sand painting. From that time on, human beings were one clan again, united by the fate the destroyers planned for all of them, for all living things ...

Leslie Marmon Silko
Excerpt from her novel *Ceremony*

Pebbles

Lying awake in the woolly dark
I watch a slash of light slip under the door
and fasten itself to the baseboard
An ancient basket hovers by my bed
There are pebbles inside, all strangely alike
slate gray and white speckled
smooth and oval like hummingbird eggs

Oh we're not eggs, they insist
We didn't steadily grow into bursting
expand into feathers and song
We came from a jumble of rock chunks
Patient, angular, we waited for water
for the raging gales and slow churning ice
the spring flushes and calm dappled currents
to size us down, to slowly O so slowly
carry us and plant us in the sea

But the tides brought us back to the shore
and now our fate is here, in your dream

Hour of the Marigold

In first morning light
a black girl comes singing past my camp
a lantern of Africa snuffing the night
Her voice fills me with such joy I wonder
why this grace for me?

Is she singing away the shame I felt
eight years old the Spring after the war
the 2nd world war, my helpless shame
when the girl from Sunday School said
my skin so dark 'cause my mama left me
in the sun too long

Is she an echo of the black nanny's
murmuring smile, the one who passed us
every day on her way to the bus up the street
Once she gave us a penny from her brown cloth purse
We were amazed and called her the penny lady
We were more amazed at the black man
who stopped to yell at us, shaking his fist
his shirt frayed at the cuffs
his grizzled head nodding up and down
I fought in the war for you, he said
I ate shit for you
We just stood there anxious
jump ropes limp in our hands

Was she the flower of days
I wandered down hill to the river
past tenements, past people speaking
languages I didn't understand
men sitting in undershirts on doorsteps
laughing and drinking beer
My father didn't sit in his undershirt
and he didn't drink beer

but he was one of them
sitting by the woodstove in the kitchen
resting his leg on a chair
while my mother changed compresses
on the angry red gash in his leg,
an accident at the mill

We brought a stray dog home that winter
gave him a bath and left him by the stove to dry
while we rushed off to buy canned dog food
at the store that gave ten cents a pound
for bacon fat, but we never could buy candy
Things were too dear for that in Bradford
Massachusetts 1946, where the river floated
bridge lights after dark and Africa's love
was a far away gleam in a mother's eye

Cross Country Sketches

Driving by Alabama cotton fields stripped bare
ditches full of cloud bits clinging to broken stems
I hear the miraculous songs a people planted there
dancing their weary away, soaring into Sunday
singing the courage that doesn't name itself

In Kansas a main street glitters with car metal
Strangers reveal their familiar with smiles
Their confident voices slide off store windows
drift inside, float over postcards of bombers and flags

In Iowa the prairie is stitched with barbed-wire
the highway mile on mile a shining scar
meadowlarks singing their hearts out
acres of silvery corn stubble marching west

For Troy Davis

We were raised in New England and liked cloudy days
The ferns in the woods understood

In the fifties we drove through Georgia
past Burma-shave signs and road stands selling pecans

past unpainted houses with refrigerators on the porch
Stove pipes scented the air with wood smoke

We saw your sisters singing their way to school
hair in tiny braids tied with bright ribbons.

Years later in the dry west we saw no clouds at all.
Day after day hot winds drove us to the river

In the prisons democracy was a bitter laugh
no match for cops or the rules of the ghetto

To pass entry, new inmates had to know ruthless
On the outside, stories of torture knocked on our doors

and our rooms were the sheltering arm of God
We hoped right 'til the end you would live, Troy

Our vigil became a world altar
blazing with candles of reasonable doubt

with belief in your innocence, with hope for reprieve
After you were gone, we placed our tears on that altar

As I fell asleep that night, your face appeared
in a ring of blue. The next day I woke at 4 a.m.

and the moon, heading west on its eternal highway
trailed a long blue cloud across the black sky

November 4, 2008

Alleluias rose round about midnight
In star lost cities and dirt lane villages
screens flashed waves of jubilation
over smoke stacked plains and ailing forests
over dammed rivers and plundered seas
A world libation, tears for the martyrs
for every heart and mind that fired a victory that day
bolts of justice in their hands

We knew the ones who shed no tears
whose dry schemes keep us from the table yet
whose well-fed cooks smear cabbage leaves
for legions of the hungry
waiting at doors flanked by armed guards
and acolytes in white frocks and steel boots

But that day we cheered for the bare feet
the chained feet that danced on Columbian shores
while leaping flames and the moist breath of song
fed dreams to the Milky Way

High Noon

Even from a distance
the granite bench felt like a gravestone
carefully placed on a grassy knoll
overlooking Onset Bay
where sailboats rocked in a phantom wind
and a ripple tide glittered high noon

Drawing near I saw it was engraved
in memory of a man named Peter
who died on 9/11

Piece of America's Heart

A young man in uniform
races across the grass
trumpet in hand
eager to play *God Bless*
in the front line
of the West Point Band

A Strange Flag

They sailed to the right of sunrise armed for war
No one knew where they would fight

On shore we were shadows milling about in the sand
uneasy, irritable, crowding each other

Would they find the enemy, would they be killed?
What would happen if they failed, and oh how long

would they be gone?   That night we dreamed
we were captives and didn't know why

And then, sooner than anyone dared hope
a ship appeared on the horizon, flying a strange flag

Notes on a Christian War

Fiends and dragons on the gargoyled eaves
Watch the dead Christ between the living thieves
                                        Alfred Lord Tennyson

Christmas 2002
The vultures thrive here
perching fifty plus in naked trees
fat black clumps sated with roadkill.
They ride the wind upriver, hunt meandering asphalt
We hunt the headlines
troops in the desert, ships in the gulf
Driving home past midnight headlights flashing
the evening's laughter gone, an ethereal voice
suspends us in a clear Bach prayer
high above the call to arms, the suffering to come
So clear and then it's over
The announcer pulls us into tomorrow
where all the purchased presents
wait beneath the purchased trees
Dawn is bleak and all day
the sun is lost in a haze of gathering tears

Easter 2003
The copper tree limbs stroll like women
young and easy down a rapture spring unfolding
their outstretched arms a nimbus of impending green
Rain falls sweetly on their smooth taut thighs
but Nature's ecstasy cannot erase the uranium
let loose in Iraq this day, no Nagasaki mushroom
just innocent flesh to burn in slow invisible fire
unless one is fated to die at once, at a checkpoint say
shot by terrorized men, trained to kill like dogs
Crusaders fill their righteous grails with oil
leave Baghdad's ancient treasure to the thieves
wrap their sacrifice in shrouds of stripes and stars

Who Were You?

Bin laden   bin laden   bin laden
even the pulpits called for your blood
and the children of Allah prayed

They said you exalted the fall
of the proud dollar's heart,
the strike at the war masters' lair
and the children of Allah trembled

You knew they would retaliate
their hypnotist ferocity
the terror of their arms
and the children of Allah mourned

Who were you, Bin Laden
and why did you bring firestorms of death
to the innocent children of Allah?

Guantanamo

The night I saw Jon Stuart's
gitmo puppet routine
I had this nightmare …
I'm walking through bright grass
with my girl and boy
still young and chasing butterflies
We wander into someone's yard.
A woman says where do you think
you're going and I apologize
She smiles thinly and I become uneasy
wishing I'd noticed the boundary
She smiles more sharply now
and leads us to a vast backyard.
Her man extols their vast property
Gardens flow over the walls
and fields roll on to the forest
But where is my boy?
I rush to the house.
and find him strapped to a chair
A man strikes his little white neck
with a bull whip

The Drone Masters

Their words are toxic seeds
and when they smile
a chill wind rises

Starry nights, clear days
funerals fall from the sky
grief in the villages

and the link between
the drone masters and my dread
is warm blood

how it pulses in the wounded
how quickly it grows cold
in the dead

Calling Mercy

The ground was cobalt blue that day
It felt like the middle of an unknown sea
The cool air might have been ice caps melting
Kindness flashed through the world kaleidoscope
two eyes at a time

In a cradle carefully rocking
new seeds were stirring
waiting for a planetary alignment
or a full moon
Some worried they were red
Oh no, a young man said
that's your left brain knocking
you need a cat scan

But instead of saving the cougars
they climbed into machines
and headed for Exodus
a great gunning mass of them
When they ran out of fuel
they went to the center of the city
in empty shopping carts
and gathered around a young woman
Mercy we're calling your name she sang
and everyone repeated
Mercy, we're calling your name

Stitching

I'm threading my needle with light, strands from stars
and the moon, from candles on altars, the tremulous auras
of leaves, zinnia haloes, the luminous veins of crystals
the phosphorescent luster of the sea
the rippling gleams of shady creeks

I need all the light I can get because I'm stitching
together the dark, heinous acts of this age
It's a ritual if you will, a gesture of forgiveness
a prayer to balance the dark and the light
by merging the Milky Way seen from the Sonora desert
on a moonless night with the blazing web of city
seen from the cabin of a midnight jet approaching Chicago

To embroider the border I'll use filaments of light
gathered from hungry eyes, eyes shining with questions
shining from sockets framed in feathers or fur or skin
shining witness to human disdain even for life that begins
when sperm meets egg and ends in clean white bone
eyes shining hope, shining fierce and gentle innocence

Every night I sew, each stitch a spark or a star
and when dawn lays its white hand on the dusky limbs
outside my window, I rise and set my work aside
It's time to greet the birds

IV

In my training, the medicine women were always asking me what I saw and what I dreamt, and they just accepted it as truth...They would work with what I had told them about my dreams by praying to change it if something bad was foretold ... If they pray on it, sometimes they can stop whatever is going to happen... They also called this "changing the face of it.

Mavis McCovey
excerpt from *Medicine Trails, A Life in Many Worlds,*
the story of her life as a medicine woman
of the Karuk Tribe of California
Recorded and edited by John F. Salter

The Alchemy of Light

Three birds perch side by side
in the oak near my door
The middle one has a fan of feathers
on top of its head,
upright from ear to ear
Backlit by a rising sun,
the feathers are flames with amethyst eyes

All morning as I ponder the dream's jeweled feathers
The sun spans the galaxy, quickens my lettuce
makes vitamin D in my skin
The sun!
The light that does not diminish with distance
that urges essence into trinities
body, mind and spirit its crucible

A maze of signals maps my afternoon
screens and speakers reporting the rush
to nowhere true, and everywhere and always
moral lightning flashing

As the sun sets
the day's reflections slowly rise
little moons I line up on a page
a motion in the human tide of praise

The Turtle

Powerful claws grab the edge of my night
a dark head rises between them, blue light in one eye
then a shell, huge and black. Its intricate design,
carved by the tides, ripples with starlight.

As the turtle and I drift into morning
a fox cub appears, patting a rock back and forth.
The rock is the color of burnt sienna
etched with an eon's white footprints.

A cleric in wire-rimmed glasses rushes by.
Columns of type fill a blank white sky
scrolling up and down so rapidly
I can't discern a single word.

After the words morph into a set of earphones
clipped to a chain link fence,
I ask the turtle what all this means.
You need pure word, she says, *pure word*

Pay Nanusurukam, Pay Nanuavahkam*
An Interpretation

Step softly on that bright moss
those speckled stones
the oily street so iridescent in the rain

It's your past you're stepping on
for the past is underneath you, not behind
you create it even as you pause

from whatever you are embracing --
a thrush choosing the darkest berries
the river rushing ninety feet below
the hungry homeless man
watching a squirrel eat a peanut

from whatever you think you're keeping out --
an apology you deemed inadequate
a bad dream, the whine of a spoiled child

With each step you don't so much
compress your past as pat it into place
tuck it into the ground of being
to mingle with the rest of matter

And what's on high
the deep blue ethers, the peaks
eagle circling, lightning waiting
sun life filtering down
This is not your future
It's the realm above

And you are a heart beat in the center
a shining motion, ever shifting
between what you place in the underside
and all that flows from above

A phrase from the Karuk, a California tribe whose ancestral lands span Eastern Humboldt and Western Sisykyou Counties.

The Language of Trees

In the dream
the solitary tree is leafless
Its naked branches form a massive oval
a maple or a live oak drinking light from all directions
But the tree has no roots, it hangs in a gray sky
a Magritte monolith, and the base of its trunk
tapers to the sharpened
point
of a
p
e
n
c
i
l

When I woke
I thought the dream might mean a writer's destiny
but over the years it became an image
of how the written word has uprooted us
how we took the language of trees
and shaved it to a narrow point of human purpose
how this is still happening, even as we speak
I mean, how much of what we say
and think, of what we *believe*
is derived from what's been written?

Before I Knew the Words

Walking down a road one morning
I come upon a parked truck
A soldier herds me toward it
using his rifle to indicate
that I should climb aboard

I don't want to get in that truck
so I change the dream
and wander into a room
where a young man
stretched out on a couch
holds a baby over his head
She's wide-eyed
listening to her father's
murmurs of delight

She turns to look at me
You know the meaning
of every word, don't you, I say
remembering the time
I knew the meaning
before I knew the words

Their Voices Came Later

After their children typed the long trail of pages
typed the planting of the forts, the burnings
the gunners on horseback with their ghost nets
the men with their gospels and prisons
their plans for the lands they would poison

After the Pageant of the Tribes
the dead and the living moving in spirals
like coils of a corn maiden's hair

After they entered the great hall of reckoning
hung with their masks and blankets
their regalia trimmed with shells and seeds
their shields adorned with feathers
painted with bear claws, flashes of
lightning, paw prints in a circle

After Liberty entered in handcuffs
and stood next to Geronimo
touching his ear with her whisper
I thought you wouldn't forgive me, he says
What is there to forgive, she asks
I couldn't stand up for you, he replies
It was the blood quantum
Oh please no, she says
I'm here to stand for you

After the drums beat softly to open the trial
and the judge masked as Coyote took his seat
and the jurors, clad in deer and elk skin
chanted a solemn prayer

Only then did the voices begin.
And the last to be conquered came first
They took my grandmother's baskets
the frail elder said, *packed them into a canoe*
A woman sat in the middle
smiling and waving over the bundles
She paid a half-breed to paddle her downriver
That's what we called them then
but they were still our children

A Silver Hum

Truth is like rain
Each drop is a mirror
that waters the ground of perception
and slakes thirsty dreams

Even when faint as a whisper
a silver hum rinsing the air,
it hushes the clatter of deceit
extends the fibers of connection
contains communal fire

For Leonard Peltier

My Life is a prayer for my people
                              Leonard Peltier

When I thought of your cell as a shrine
and placed a candle there
cells across the earth rose up before me
And so it began
the lighting of the candles
the placing of them cell by cell
tracing with flames
the map of political prisons
made in America

And then four symbols appeared
a nail, a tear, a crust of bread, a cross
and it seemed that the nail was the jailer
and the tear Yeat's *pity of love
beyond all telling,* and the crust of bread
was disdain beyond all telling
let them eat crust, it seemed to be saying

and the cross, which was upright, fell over
Its arms became equal in length
became the center of a fiery wheel
rolling faster and faster
over a long dark plain

Mortal in the Forest

The smell of grief on clear-cut ground
is sticky with human need, with hungers
that fasten men's hands to a chain saw
that harden their hearts to any agony of trees
And seasons of rain don't wash it away
Downpour and drizzle seep through
the sawdust, the piles of woody debris
and the animals leave their tracks

And where is the medicine
for humans who kill without reverence

In the wooden cup Spirit handed him
Black Elk saw the sky reflected in the water
Take this cup, Spirit said
it is the power to make life for your people
And take this bow and arrow
for all beings must take life to live
But when Black Elk was old
he said he'd been too weak to use these gifts

We could tell him otherwise
We could show him *our* cup
made of metal and empty now
crushed into the lip of a stone
that cradles the stars

For without that reflection of sky
the chainsaw is to the tree
what the bullet is to the heart
and grief doesn't wash away
and stars keep sending their messages
to the stone that cradles our crumpled cup
And the animals leave their tracks

Opalescent Mirrors

Disks of abalone shell drift through the void
opalescent mirrors of the moon
An azure blue garden hose slithers around them
a strange snake with the garish finish of plastic dye
No water drips from the hose

Is this our goodbye to eternity,
remnants of ancient regalia
and the menacing coils of a technology
that has drained the wellsprings of our Soul?

Climate Icons

On a backyard altar made of cinder blocks
two fat white candles sit in folds of wax
flames barely stir

A bamboo cutting with one green leaf
roots in a jar of muddy water
There's a hawk feather and wilted marigolds

Nearby some hens eye an empty rabbit hutch
on top of which another candle burns
as if this too were an altar

Nearby a pair of sunglasses glitters in dry grass
one lens missing, the other cracked
the frame twisted at the bridge

Hovering over all is the shadow of a bear
Her dark silhouette glows pale and gray
has a powdery mist at the edge

The Lobster

I'm on the edge of a cliff
confronted by a mammoth thrashing lobster
Its claws are bigger than I am
A sheer wall of rock towers behind it
If he makes a move, I could go over the edge
My daughter appears
I don't know if she has come to help
or bear witness
It may be evening
It may be that the lobster
just wants to return to the sea

Sipping as One

I
Even in a drought I can take a shower
wash my dishes, water the garden
drink all the water I want
Every simple ordinary day I can do this
because I live within the heart of empire
in a place where water's still safe

But I've seen the photographs
the long dusty lines near the water trucks
Men, women, children
waiting with plastic and metal containers
waiting for the gallon or two
that will get them through the day
I've seen Africa's bony animals
at dried-up water holes
the dead fish above a shrinking water line
the scorched fields
the girls walking hours for water

I know Asia's largest inland sea
is a ghost of its former self
the worry of sea level rise
the global battles over water
the corporate grab for water
And it's hard not to feel incensed
that anyone thinks they can own water

To heal this is a daily prayer
It is also a memory that reaches back
to the beginning of human time here
A memory of how it was before the pipes
before the conduits, before the weapons
that enabled empires
to disable life's access to water

A memory of the ancient understanding
that we must serve All Alive
in all we do

II
I turn on the faucet and fill a cup with water
imagining the life that might be mine
if I filled it from a Spring outside my door
or drank from a wild mountain stream

I think how it's still a Being, even after the pipes
How it rises from the silky tension of pond skin
how it becomes lily breath and rides the wind
shifts from mist into cloud

How it mirrors the sun, spreading its spectrum
across the sky, how it becomes a soft rain
or a deluge pelting earth, how it slips down walls
filters through loam and rock
finds the hollows underground
seeps into wells and marshes
bubbles up into springs

I think of how minutely it flows in every cell
and imagine every being on Earth
plants, animals, fishes, birds and insects
all of us, sipping as one

Why There is Laughter

The indigenous women in rural Mexico
have no use for the NGO's energy efficient stoves
They explain it simply enough
A family needs fire at its center
Kettles must balance on three stones

They have no use for the water tower either
They like to walk down to the pool
where they can honor Spirit
Maybe that is why there is laughter
when they carry full jugs uphill on their heads

The trappings of civilization
they seem to be saying are traps.
What happens they wonder
to those who drink water from pipes
Some of us could tell them and if we did
they would puzzle all the more

The Quail Are Frolicking On My Roof

as if my tears contain no salt
and now in gathering sweetness glide
into clear jade currents of spring

as if past wrongs can be made right
and the earth child's sparkle-eyed smile
had never been smashed

as if healing is a certain truth
beyond the clanging chain of days
caught in perversity's tailwind

and the lupine's sheer ebullient blue
the nodding milkmaid's pale perfume
can clear away yesterday's shadows

The Mandrill

It's late afternoon at a sprawling market
in Equatorial Guinea, not many people about
a few strollers, farmers closing up their stalls.
A merchant who deals in bush animals
sits under a lone shade tree, a boy at his side.
Nearby a mandrill, tethered to a post
on an eight-foot metal chain, is stretched out flat.
His arms reach over his head into the dirt road,
hands limp in the dust.
He looks puzzled, desperate, pleading.
Behind the merchant are wire mesh cages.
Each contains a crouching monkey.
All have been sold to a laboratory.
The mandrill is being sold for meat.

A European couple passing by
stop and stare at the mandrill, aghast.
Their impulse is to help him.
Doesn't the mandrill need water they ask.
Water is scarce and costly in the dusty market
and the merchant has none to spare.
It's then they notice the caged monkeys.
Again their impulse is to help
but the merchant is aroused now.
He has picked up on their judgment, that they
think him cruel.   His tone has a guarded edge
when he again explains he has no water.

The woman shows him her water bottle,
asks for a bowl or a cup.
The merchant shakes his head.

The couple, having decided
to buy the mandrill and release it,
set off in search of a truck.

Meanwhile, the mandrill has drifted into a dream
deep in the forest, high in a tree with the birds,
with their bright feathers and bright songs
and the monkey's bright chatter.

When the couple returns for the mandrill.
they find it has passed out.
The merchant pokes it to no avail.
It should be in the shade, the woman says.
The merchant agrees and again tries to rouse
the mandrill who still does not respond.
Afraid he'll lose the sale, the merchant shakes him.
The animal opens his eyes but remains inert.

The woman offers the mandrill a tin of water.
He takes a sip.

A Fly Story

I saved a fly today
not to spare her a drowning
but to get her out of my tea
To my surprise, she deftly climbed
the matchstick I was using to remove her
then wobbled up onto my finger

I tried to blow her off
but she didn't budge
so I blew harder
She hung on
Finally I shook my hand.
and she tumbled to the ground
stumbled in the dust, righted herself
and headed off in the direction
of the porch step, listing a bit
from the extra ballast
of creamy tea droplets and dust motes

Her direction seemed deliberate.
Was she headed for that trapezoid
of sunlight created by the shadows
of the five-trunk walnut tree?
She stopped in the shade
climbed onto a leaf and shook
Then she wiped her wings with
her feet a few times and headed
straight for the patch
of drying light
Once there she continued along
her sunlit trajectory
eventually to mount a ridge of dirt
formed by yesterday's raking.

Once there she cleaned her wings again
fanned them a few times, and continued
Before she reached the end
of the sun patch however
which was two and a half feet long
she went airborne
into the door we'd left open.
Bemused at the thought
of her buzzing around the rooms later
I decided to write this poem
at which point I realized
that when she annoyed me
by falling into my tea
I thought of her as male
but when she confirmed
my hunch she'd go for the light
I thought of her as female

Maybe I identified with her
attraction to the sun
maybe I wanted to defy
male dominion one more time
Maybe I wanted to invoke the mother
of all creatures who seek the light,
the ultimate Mother
who decides if we live or die
as Leslie Mormon Silko tells it
in her story of the long-ago time
when the green bottlefly
saved the people from drought
by asking the Mother of the People
to forgive them the harm they'd done
a wrong that caused
the plants and animals to disappear

A Cesium Sea

The late winter wind sings an anthem of green
a singular tune about life without cruelty
where all the mobbed and intricate realms
of human endeavor gone mad
are drowned in a spice gold cesium sea
lost forever and ever, which never were anyway
but for the warm stirring wind
the birthing rain, the pulsing light
blessing over and over the stone ground stone
the lush rotted mast, the velvet dust
the thirsty scattered seed

V

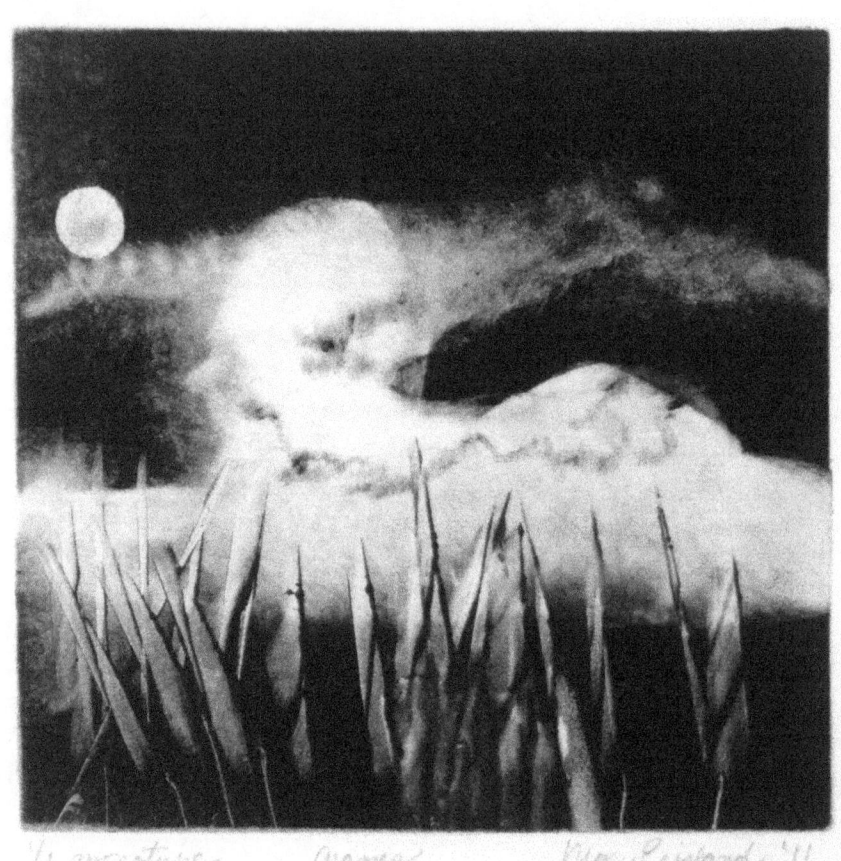

Again and again.
The earth is new again.
They come, listen, listen.
Hold on to your mother's hand.
They come.

O great joy, they come.
the plants with bells.
The stones with voices.

Simon Ortiz,
excerpt from *Earth and Rain, The Plants & Sun*

Waking up in the Infinite Plan

O intricate I almost missed
wrapped in warm sheets of thought
The beaded branches quaking
The creek with its strong winter riff
The new roof tasting its first snow

Her Lichen Eyes

Approaching Dragon Rock
the eager April air contagious as laughter
I watch last night's rain skip with snowmelt
down the creek that flows between us

I call to her from a small clearing in the pines
asking for guidance
Her answers drift over the dappled current
As the words sound in my mind
I no longer fear I'm making them up
because they are so unexpected and feel true

When I shift my stance, her lichen eyes follow
I'm amazed at this, amazed she can see me
wherever I stand

Sometimes we talk over the water
Sometimes, gripping branches for support
finding toeholds in the roots
I climb down the steep bank, slosh over gravel
and slippery rocks to be near her
When I'm close enough to kneel, I only listen

To Tongore Creek

What can I give you little river
for singing as you gather
lightfall unto water bound
last night's blue gold star waves
the green glow surrounding the moon
dawn's peach glaze upon the snow

for your cobalt swirl through
tinkling caverns of turquoise ice
and all around the frozen light,
pine needle icicles glistening
branches wrapped in glass
opal eyes winking

all this light, little river
so soon to join your wet laughter
even as shadows spread their pools
of pale blue ink on soft white fields
slowing the snow melt only so long,
before it seeps into your song
your jubilee always song
for the wedding of water and light

Tso'noma Song

O you day of squalls and sun, you pelting
rushes of rain that suddenly slow into shimmers
of airborne dew, a drop or two touching
my face and everywhere dazzles of silver
and green, and a wanton carrying on between
lush new leaves and drenched-into-bold
exuberant grass, clouds coming and going
in a blue forever and the ground so drenched
little ponds gleam in the vineyards and line
the bike trail with smiling sheets of sky,
enchanting the land even as new drops fly in
front runners for a swift moving cloud god
soon to erase his tourmaline halo
and let loose with a fresh load of rain

Tso'noma is a word of the Miwok, Pomo and Wintun peoples and was the name of a chief with a big nose, considered a sign of leadership. It and has been translated as Valley of the Moon and as a place tag, similar in usage to the 'burgs or 'villes of European languages.

Insectival Buzz

Sometimes the fine hum of a hazy summer day
sounds the same inside and out
all the windows open, ears bathed in an ether
of steady mild soprano

No cars go by, no power tools, only the huff
of a door closing on the other side of the blackberries
and the rooster out back,
pausing in the middle of a muted call

A couple of crows toss a few muffled caws into the
day's song, if that's what this is
this lake of air, this shimmering insectival buzz
that ripples with each new drop of sound

Now it's three keen cries, half squawk, half squeek
uttered from the moist percussive
throat of a scrub jay defining his domain
from a perch on my bean pole

Diary with Lime and Magenta

La Jolla was the sea blue end of a long drive west
where next packed away with *no turning back*
It was warm winter days and raked sand
barefoot runs in low hushing surf
ocean air easing muscle and mind
releasing their knots to the flowering streets
eyes drawn like bees to the glow of magenta
That's how it was until the jasmine bloomed
teasing my brain into restless
even as the scent of cistus held me fast
and pulled me back, into a scent of sweet fern
a Mt. Wachusetts meadow
Mary picking berries glazed with light
my brothers' plump fists in her pail
my sisters and I climbing lime lichen boulders
Little godlings we were, with blue mouths
Joseph turned in to the Red Sox...

Driving north on Route 1
I followed crimson clover chimes
and marched with a brass band of blue flag
fan-faring away in a roadside field
then on to a lair of foxglove
a meadow of mimulus humming hymns to the sea
a bench where streams of late-day sun
turned petals of magenta
into the rose pink glow my lost heart loved
That night I fell asleep to a lone trumpet
another camper off in the Redwoods somewhere

In Orleans the live oaks sighed
stay here they sighed, stay here
Stay with these naked madrones
with their crinkly strips of rust-orange skin
and that pigmy owl out in broad daylight
watching you walk a narrow cliff road
lined with quivering rattle grass

So I stayed and found a river as restless as my mind
I watched that swift glassy river
how it poured over boulders
curled back in perpetual rustles of foam
On the shore dwarf lupines hummed the ineffable
their blue notes lilting, rippling down the bar
I strolled the elfin grass there, red blades
tipped in lime, past streams of billowing vetch
almost giddy in purple, past waves of owl clover
straight into the arms of beatitude
I was Monet, Bonnard, Gaughin, rapt forever
or might have been if an arc of wild pea magenta
hadn't pulled my eye to the rickrack horizon
the clear cut strips, the tinder dry remnants of forest
saying yes, yes what happened to us is what
happened to you -- something sacred plundered
Thousands of acres burned that year
but when I took to the road again
fire sprouts were thriving and the slopes
were whistling green, lime green, and charcoal black

In the Catskills the forests were closets of rain
When they opened their doors the creeks ran wild
and all around the voices rang
By night the owls and coyotes, by day the songbirds
the squirrels and jays, hummingbirds whizzing
and the soft drone of bees
The leaves let loose on their chloroplast drums
heart beats in an oxygen sea
High chords of berry magenta tuned in
and lime yellow pond lilies warbled in D
It was all a brilliant ephemeral
those resonant coils of infinity's hair
those God brimming lanterns of color
a communion of sunlight, water and air
and me, happily singing in bondage
to plant breath and being aware

Klamath River Tao

It's the way the morning vapors shift
slow motion echo of stream flow
trailing to eddies, curling to wisps
drifting up the valley's sheerdown blue

The way the current emerges from winter
bounding baritone the whole night long
gathering days of rain from gravid streams
gorging on sandbars and rock piles

The way the sun rays sip the dew
from silver leaves.
You'd think those blister tears
the sad ones shed would shy themselves away
in the face of such largesse

But grief endures,   once-vast forests cling
for dear life to steep berried slopes, even as
helicopters graze with ill intent, still to feed
the Grand Inquisitor greed that cut our cord
to the heart that holds the world together

It's the way the Karuk sang their prayers
each Spring to shine the salmon upriver
The way they dance yet to renew this world

It's the way a small covey of birders
aim their binoculars, hushed and alert, hoping
to catch a glimpse of a ruby-crowned kinglet
so tiny a cap of ethereal red, so brilliant a patch
for that long-ago severed connection

Rain Woman

She wakes me at four in the morning
although the mad drumming that breaks my sleep
is more the resistance of corrugated fiberglass
than the wild velocity of her downpour.

I'm on the porch, zipped into a sleeping bag.
She's glissading in sheets around the porch.
The roof is running interference
and as the saying goes, three's a crowd.

I want to hear her, only her.
I want to listen with my feathered head
tucked in a downy wing, to be warm
and dry in my den, ears alert

eyes staring into the wet dark. I want to hear
how she eases silver into velvet moss
how she spatters the duff, pummels dusty leaves
so I get up and walk into the storm.

Just before dawn, she disappears.
I become a leaf shedding her shining
a blade of grass silently sipping
a very cold stone

In the Canyon

All day in the canyon, voices on voices
the Buddha of Harmony, humming

And because it was April
the Trillium wore dark red robes

The birds trailed bright little flags
in and out of fluted fluttering leaves

When chattering hikers came through
their voices fell like coins on a spiderweb

And so the day passed
When the shadows began their eastward shift

the birds finished posting their prayers
to the Invisibles

With darkness came the owls, and all night
wild ferns bathed in Buddha's cool breath

Their Wings Made No Sound

They were there again
Every day they sang in the trees
but this day was different
The birds came into her room
and their wings made no sound
The sleeping dogs did not even stir

Why are you here, she sighed
Just stretch out your arms
the flycatcher replied, I need a perch
It was a kind deception
meant to help her open wide
what had long been closed

And she did open
and knew the feel of bird feet on her skin
saw close the soft pink underwing
the dark line from the tip of his beak
to his bright black eye
and a wave of light flowed up her spine

Animal Trust

A dragon touched my cheek today
and now I want to be a breeze
mild and sweet with apple scent
brushing his scales so lightly
he doesn't know if it's me
or his imagination

And I want to share
the apples when they fall
before any bruise appears
relishing the one body
the soil, the tree
the blossom, the bee
living in animal trust
as written by the very hand
that sent that dragon fire
into my puddle of rain

Love Song in A Minor

for my seventh decade, death a familiar now
and life a bursting seed in the never-old play
of light and shade in the everywhere somewhere
water flows, in the veins of a burgundy trillium say
April's tracery, encasing sips of sun and air
easing trails of scent into infinite morning
dreams waving every which way
from the mind, the trees, a gay yellow beak
trilling intricate avian alchemies
peals of instinct and air that end the instant
the robin's aware I discovered her nest
and I almost regret my feather-craving eyes
added a quake of alarm to her warrior gaze
like the flightless owl, whose eyes flare wide
when my stranger hand opens his cage
not fooled when I looked away
oh no, defiant and glaring for stronger proof
it's love I offer this day

In Full Leaf

Every day for a week
I have the same silent dream
I'm sitting on the porch in West Shokan
spring trees in full leaf
still bright but past their lively lime unfolding
faintly edged with hints of flame

The silence seems all silk and air
or maybe not silence at all but light
arms of light, reaching through the trees
to open the door, let in the birds
the murmuring streets, the whispering trees
long past their lively lime unfolding
faintly edged with hints of flame

Petals

I cast the petals of each day
to sun and moon and pray me brave
Holding fast to each clear moment
every cup of air, I kneel in velvet dusk
to plant another season's seeds
After fifty years it seems a sacred act
an ancient way of giving thanks
A ceremony honed in thunder, rain and light
A new day prayer for you and me
and old coyote who never stops watching
holding fast to all we've lost
A quickening prayer for the soil
the sprouts, the bees
A healing prayer for the wounded
grief in the bone
for green and water renewing
the luminous flow of all alive
together and alone

Acknowledgements

I owe deep thanks to many friends for their support over the years this book has been evolving. Marcia Newfield, Helen Weaver and Mike Tuggle gave detailed edits to an early version. Their thoughtful suggestions encouraged me to persevere. Intuitive suggestions from John Miatech and Mary Prisland were invaluable. Comments from Sandy Eastoak, Gwynn O'Gara and Hale Thatcher contributed to a final winnowing. I am grateful to my sisters Claire Pratt and Carole DuPre for their generous support. And to Jim Ferrara for his explanations of Karuk myths and stories.

I am profoundly grateful to Evan Pritchard, whose careful reading and eloquent endorsement are a blessing any writer would wish for.

Special thanks to Mary Prisland for her art and Michael Sterne for his photographs of her images.

About the Artists

Mary Prisland

The etching monotypes introducing each section are by Mary Prisland, who grew up in Wisconsin and found her true home when she moved to Northern California in her twenties in 1972. A psychologist and an artist, Mary's portraits probe interior dreamscapes. Her landscapes explore the numinous realms of Nature. Her comment on *'Native American with Child' (page 20):*

"When I began this etching, I had no image at all in my mind, no thought of what it would be. As I lay the ink on the plate, the images emerged. To this day their source is a mystery."

Carole DuPre

The cover design was done by Carole Dupre. The photograph of Dragon Rock, the subject of the poem *Lichen Eyes*, was taken by the author.

Cynthia Poten

was born and raised in New England, found Manhattan after college, and eventually migrated to rural New Jersey to raise her two children. She has been an office assistant, puppeteer, gardener, free-lance writer, visiting home-maker and the first Delaware Riverkeeper. She lives near Sebastopol, CA where she works as a substitute teacher and as a producer for KIDE Hoopa Tribal Radio. Her radio productions include the four-hour documentary *Being Indian in America* and *What They are Saying, The Hearts and Minds of U.S. Veterans.*

Her poems have been published by *Chronogram, The Anderson Valley News, The Big River Poetry Anthology,* and on-line by poetrylovers@lists.sonic.net. This is her first book.

To contact: cypoten@gmail.com.

www.ingramcontent.com/pod-product-compliance
Lightning Source LLC
Chambersburg PA
CBHW032139040426
42449CB00005B/323